WE CAN DRAW

WE CAN DRAW
DOGS

Corina Jeffries

WINDMILL BOOKS™

New York

Published in 2023 by Windmill Books, an Imprint of Rosen Publishing
29 East 21st Street, New York, NY 10010

Portions of this work were originally authored by Laura Murawski and published as *How to Draw Dogs*. All new material this edition authored by Corina Jeffries.

Library of Congress Cataloging-in-Publication Data
Names: Jeffries, Corina, author.
Title: We can draw dogs / Corina Jeffries.
Description: New York : Windmill Books, [2023] | Series: We can draw |
   Includes index. | Audience: Grades 2-3
Identifiers: LCCN 2021059106 (print) | LCCN 2021059107 (ebook) | ISBN
   9781508198147 (library binding) | ISBN 9781508198123 (paperback) | ISBN
   9781508198130 (set) | ISBN 9781508198154 (ebook)
Subjects: LCSH: Dogs in art–Juvenile literature. |
   Drawing–Technique–Juvenile literature.
Classification: LCC NC783.8.D64 J44 2023 (print) | LCC NC783.8.D64
   (ebook) | DDC 743.6/9772–dc23/eng/20220106
LC record available at https://lccn.loc.gov/2021059106
LC ebook record available at https://lccn.loc.gov/2021059107

Designer: Leslie Taylor
Editor: Caitie McAneney

Photo credits: Cover, p. 1 (dog) Ammit Jack/Shutterstock.com; series cover artwork (pencils) suriya yapin/Shutterstock.com; series cover artwork (art table) insta_photos/Shutterstock.com; series cover artwork (banner) Kathy Kiselova/Shutterstock.com; series cover artwork (scribbles) mart/Shutterstock.com; p. 4 Holly S Cannon/Shutterstock.com; p. 5 (pencils) ILLUSTOR STUDIO/Shutterstock.com; p. 5 (girl and boy) Monkey Business Images/Shutterstock.com; p. 6 Jef Wodniack/Shuttertstock.com; p. 8 Natalia Fedosova/Shutterstock.com; p. 10 art nick/Shutterstock.com; p. 12 MindStorm/Shuttertstock.com; p. 14 Daniele COSSU/Shutterstock.com; p. 16 Yuri Kravchenko/Shutterstock.com; p. 18 Kasefoto/Shutterstock.com; p. 20 tsik/Shuttertstock.com.

Manufactured in the United States of America

CPSIA compliance information: Batch #CSWM23: For further information contact Rosen Publishing, New York, New York at 1-800-237-9932.

Find us on

CONTENTS

DRAWING DIFFERENT DOGS

Dogs have been loyal friends to humans for thousands of years. Throughout history, they were used for many different jobs, such as herding and hunting. Now, they're usually just a person's best friend!

There are around 360 dog **breeds** around the world. Some are big, and some are small. Some have long hair, and some have short hair. In this book, you'll learn about seven different breeds of dogs, as well as their **ancestor**—the gray wolf. As you draw, you'll notice how dogs compare to the gray wolf. You'll also notice how different breeds have different kinds of fur. Drawing different kinds of fur takes practice, but you'll learn a lot as you try new **techniques**. Let's start drawing dogs!

First, you'll learn how to draw a gray wolf. The dogs we have as pets today share many **traits** with the wild gray wolf. As you continue to learn how to draw new breeds of dogs, you'll notice how they are all similar in some ways. Follow the instructions step by step as you create your canines!

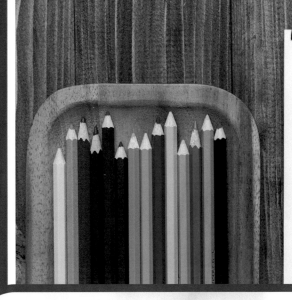

Gather your drawing materials!

You'll need a pencil, pencil sharpener, eraser, and paper. You might want to make your drawings in a sketch pad.

LET'S DRAW A GRAY WOLF!

The history of dogs starts with the gray wolf. Researchers long believed that the wolf was tamed by humans about 12,000 years ago. However, wolves may have actually started **evolving** into dogs about 130,000 years ago. Many traits of the gray wolf are seen in dogs today. Two of these traits are being loyal and being great hunters.

The gray wolf could once be found all over the world. Unfortunately, people started hunting the gray wolf and damaging the lands where it lived. From the 1970s to the 2010s, gray wolves were protected in the United States. This helped their numbers rise, which helped **ecosystems**. However, loosened hunting laws in states such as Montana, Wisconsin, and Idaho are hurting wolf populations once again.

Conservation efforts helped gray wolves build their populations again in some places, like Yellowstone National Park.

1

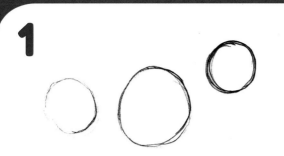

First, draw three circles like the ones shown in the illustration. Notice where they are placed on the page and their different sizes.

2

Connect the circles with curved lines to form the body of the gray wolf as shown.

3

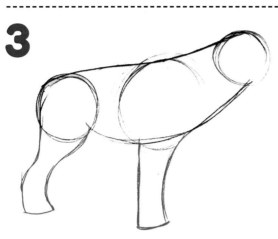

To form the legs of the gray wolf, draw the two shapes shown in the illustration.

4

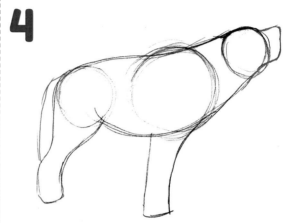

Now, draw in the shape of the snout in the front and the shape of the tail in the back.

5

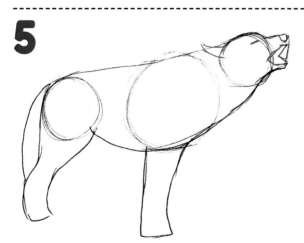

Add some detail to the head by drawing the ear, the eye, the nose, and the mouth.

6

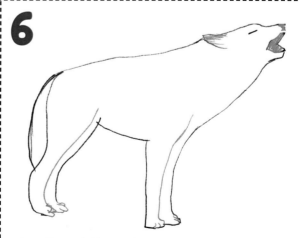

Lastly, add lines to complete the legs as shown. Erase any extra lines. Shade the mouth and ear. Your gray wolf will look like this!

LET'S DRAW A SALUKI!

One of the oldest existing dog breeds in the world is the saluki. This dog's history dates back to ancient Sumer and Egypt, more than 4,000 years ago. The saluki was an important dog in ancient Egypt, where it was highly respected. Images of salukis have been found in paintings and on carvings and pottery across Egypt, Asia, and parts of Europe.

Salukis generally have smooth fur, with longer, fluffier fur on the ears and tail. They are built tall and lean. Males can reach 28 inches (71.1 cm) tall and can weigh up to 70 pounds (31.8 kg). Originally a hunting dog, salukis run very fast and are always up for a chase. The saluki's long legs give the dog grace and speed while running.

The saluki was known as "El Hor," or "the noble one," in ancient Egypt.

1

First, draw three circles like the ones shown in the illustration. Notice where they are placed on the page and their different sizes.

2

Connect the circles with curved lines to form the body of the saluki as shown.

3

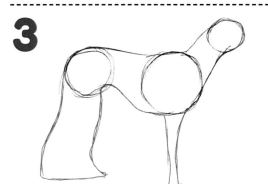

To form the front and back legs of the saluki, draw the two shapes as shown.

4

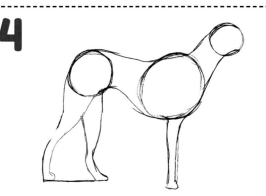

Draw in two curved lines as shown to finish the back legs.

5

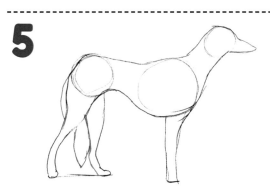

Next, draw in the shape of the snout in the front and the tail in the back. Notice how the saluki's tail falls between the two back legs.

6

Now, draw in the face. Draw an ear, an eye, the nose, and the mouth.

7

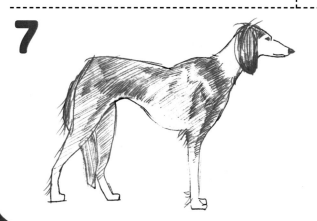

Lastly, you can erase any extra lines and color in the coat of the saluki by shading your drawing as shown. To make the soft look of the coat, shade line by line. That's one super saluki!

LET'S DRAW
A CHIHUAHUA!

Chihuahuas are tiny dogs with big ears! The Chihuahua is one of the smallest types of dog. The chihuahua gets its name from a state in Mexico. The breed is believed to come from a dog known as the techichi, which can be traced back to the ninth century in Mexico. This dog is considered the first of the chihuahua breed.

Commonly, chihuahuas weigh between 3 and 6 pounds (1.4 and 2.7 kg). That's smaller than a cat! Their heads are shaped like apples. They can have long or short fur. Chihuahuas are very loyal, smart, and quick to learn. They love to be with their owners, and some people even carry their chihuahuas around with them wherever they go.

Chihuahuas can have different hair lengths and colors. You'll be drawing a chihuahua with short hair.

1

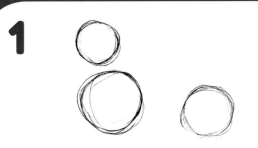

First, draw three circles like the ones shown in the illustration. Notice where they are placed on the page and their different sizes.

2

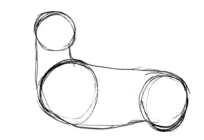

Connect the circles with curved lines to form the body of the chihuahua as shown.

3

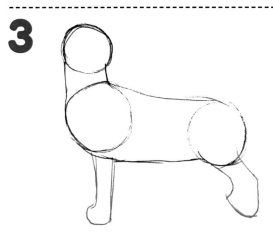

To form the legs, draw the two shapes shown above.

4

Next, draw two triangles on the top circle for the ears. Draw the tail in the back.

5

Draw the eyes, the nose, and the mouth. Draw a curved line to finish the back legs and a tiny paw peeking out from behind the front leg as shown.

6

Now, you can erase any extra lines. Lastly, add some shading to your drawing. To make the fur look wavy and soft, shade line by line. Your chihuahua might look like this!

LET'S DRAW A DALMATIAN!

You may have seen dalmatians in the Disney movie *One Hundred and One Dalmatians*. They're a breed of dog that's easy to spot. That's because they are born all white, but as they grow, they become covered in dark spots!

People don't know for sure where dalmatians are from. Some believe that they came from an area called Dalmatia in Eastern Europe, which is how they got their name. They were often working dogs. In England in the 1600s, for example, dalmatians often helped out at firehouses. In those days, fire "trucks" were actually horse-drawn carriages. To help the firemen, a dalmatian would run ahead of the carriage and bark to clear the way. These dogs are often athletic and need plenty of exercise.

In history, dalmatians were often watchdogs, tasked with guarding horses and coaches. Today, they are still loyal and protective.

1 First, draw three circles like the ones shown in the illustration. Notice where they are placed on the page and their different sizes.

2 Connect the circles with curved lines to form the body of the dalmatian as shown.

3 Next, draw the two shapes shown here to form the front and back legs.

4 Now, draw the ear and snout in the front and the shape of the tail at back.

5 Look to the illustration as you add lines to fill in the legs.

6 Draw the eyes, the nose, and the mouth. Add details to the paws, and erase extra lines.

7 Lastly, you can draw in the spots to make a dashing dalmatian.

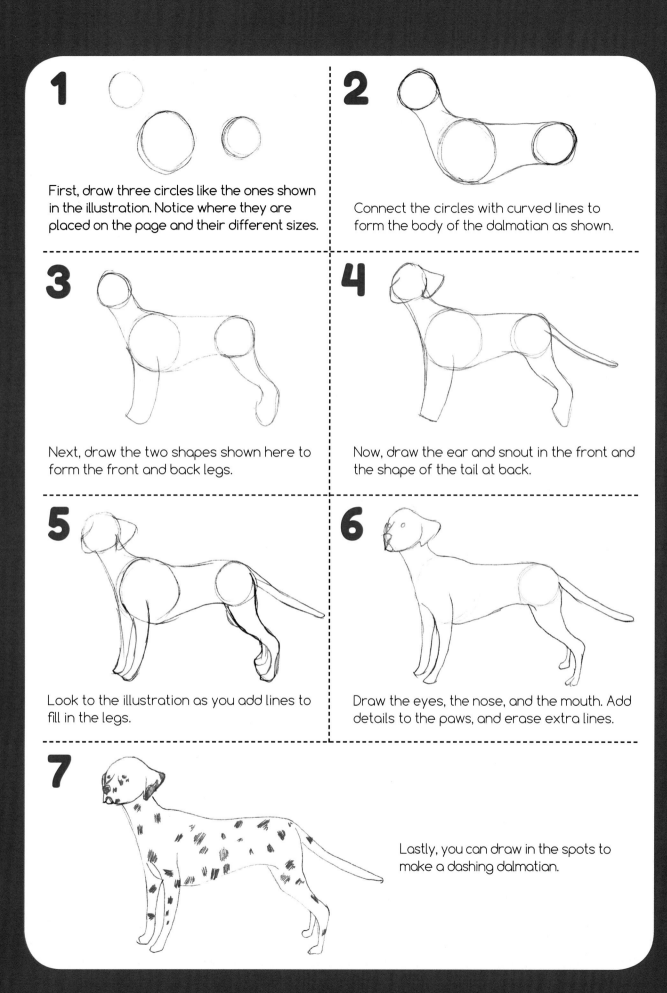

LET'S DRAW
A GOLDEN RETRIEVER!

Golden retrievers are common family pets in the United States. These dogs are gentle, fun-loving, loyal, and easy to train. They are also known for their beautiful golden coats. They love to run and swim. Many like to play catch with their owners since they were originally bred to retrieve ducks and other water birds for hunters.

Golden retrievers were first raised as hunting dogs in Great Britain. They are called retrievers because they like to hunt and to carry things in their mouths. Golden retrievers came to America from Europe in 1925. Before long, they became popular house pets. Because they are easy to train, some golden retrievers help guide and support people with special needs. Today, families all over the world love their golden retrievers.

Golden retrievers don't all look the same. Some have light hair, and some have darker hair.

1

First, draw three circles like the ones shown in the illustration. Notice where they are placed on the page and their different sizes.

2

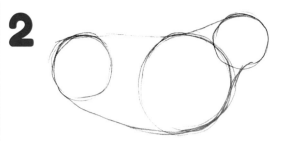

Connect the circles with curved lines to form the body of the golden retriever as shown.

3

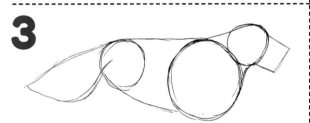

Next, draw a square shape for the snout in the front. Draw the curved shape of the tail in the back.

4

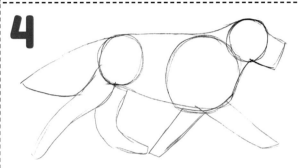

For the legs, draw four shapes under the body that look like rectangles with curved sections.

5

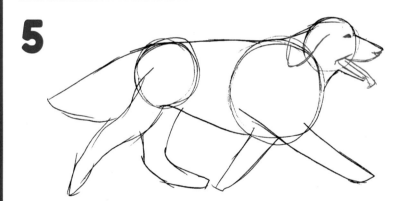

Draw the eye, the nose, the mouth (with the tongue out), and the ear.

6

You can erase any extra lines. Lastly, shade in your drawing. To make the fur look soft and wavy, shade line by line. Your golden retriever will look like this one!

LET'S DRAW A BASENJI!

The basenji is one of the oldest breeds around today. In fact, some scientists say that the first dogs to be **domesticated** probably looked like basenjis. The basenji originated in Central Africa and was sent to ancient Egypt. The basenji was mostly used as a hunting dog in Africa. It has very good eyesight and a terrific sense of smell. Basenjis came to England in the 1930s and the United States about 50 years later.

The basenji is known as the "barkless dog." It does not bark like other dogs. Instead, it makes **yodeling** and growling sounds. Basenjis have short fur and a curly tail. Basenjis clean themselves by licking their fur, especially around their face, like a cat.

Basenjis are very active dogs that need plenty of exercise.

1

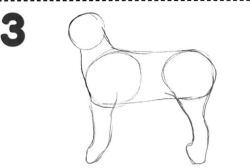

First, draw three circles like the ones shown in the illustration. Notice where they are placed on the page and their different sizes.

2

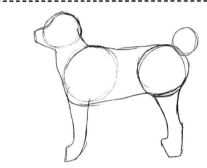

Connect the circles with curved lines to form the body of the basenji as shown here.

3

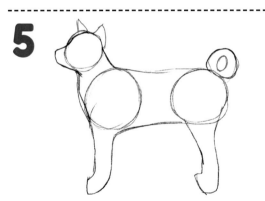

Next, draw two shapes as shown to form the front and back legs of the basenji.

4

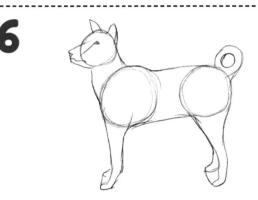

Draw in the shape of the snout in the front. Draw a circle for the curled tail in the back.

5

Then, draw two curved triangles to make the ears. Draw another small circle inside the circle you drew for the tail.

6

Draw an eye, the nose, and the mouth for the face. Add lines to complete the legs as shown here.

7

You can erase any extra lines. Shade in the ears, an eye, the nose, and the tail. What a beautiful basenji!

LET'S DRAW
A BEAGLE!

Beagles are a favorite dog to keep as a pet. Though they were bred to hunt, they're often happy to just spend time at home with their people. The beagle's **personality** is a big reason why it is so popular. Beagles are playful, loyal, and smart.

Beagles were bred for the hunt. They have special skills and senses. For example, beagles are very good at sniffing out **prey**. A beagle can sniff out a rabbit hours after it's gone from sight. Because of their great sense of smell, beagles have been used as scent-detecting dogs at airports. Instead of bombs or drugs, many beagles are used to find food and plants that are being brought into a country illegally. Beagles are mainly led by their noses when they play too.

Beagles have long ears—which help them smell! Their long ears catch smells in the air and keep them close to their nose.

1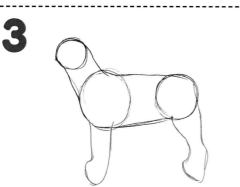

First, draw three circles like the ones shown in the illustration. Notice where they are placed on the page and their different sizes.

2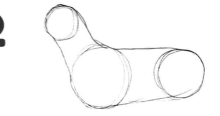

Connect the circles with curved lines to form the body of the beagle as shown.

3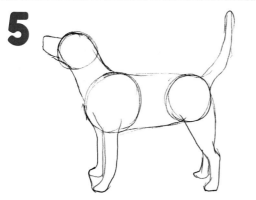

Next, draw two shapes to form the front and back legs of the beagle as shown.

4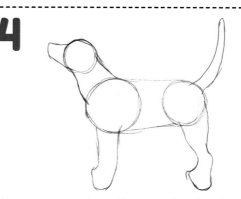

You can now draw the snout in the front and the tail in the back.

5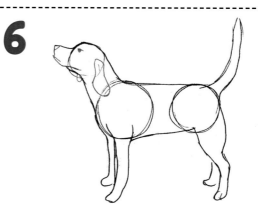

Now, finish the front and back legs by drawing in curved lines as shown.

6

Draw an eye, the nose, the mouth, and an ear to make the face.

7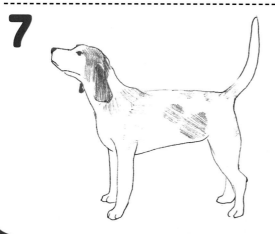

You can now erase any extra lines. Lastly, you can shade in the markings of the beagle. To make the look of the wavy coat, shade line by line. That beagle looks brilliant!

LET'S DRAW A BOXER!

Another popular dog breed is the boxer. While their name might sound tough, boxers are known to be loyal, loving, and smart. This muscular dog got its name from the way it raises its paws like a human boxer when it plays or fights. Standing up to 25 inches (58 cm) tall and weighing up to 80 pounds (36.3 kg), the boxer is a very playful dog.

Boxers are known for being hard-working and good with people. They have a great sense of smell and excellent hearing. Throughout history, these qualities have been useful to their human companions. There are many stories of boxers helping people by sniffing out danger or protecting their homes. Because they like to protect their owners, boxers make great guard dogs.

The boxer is recognized by its pointy ears, muscular body, big eyes, and wrinkled head.

1

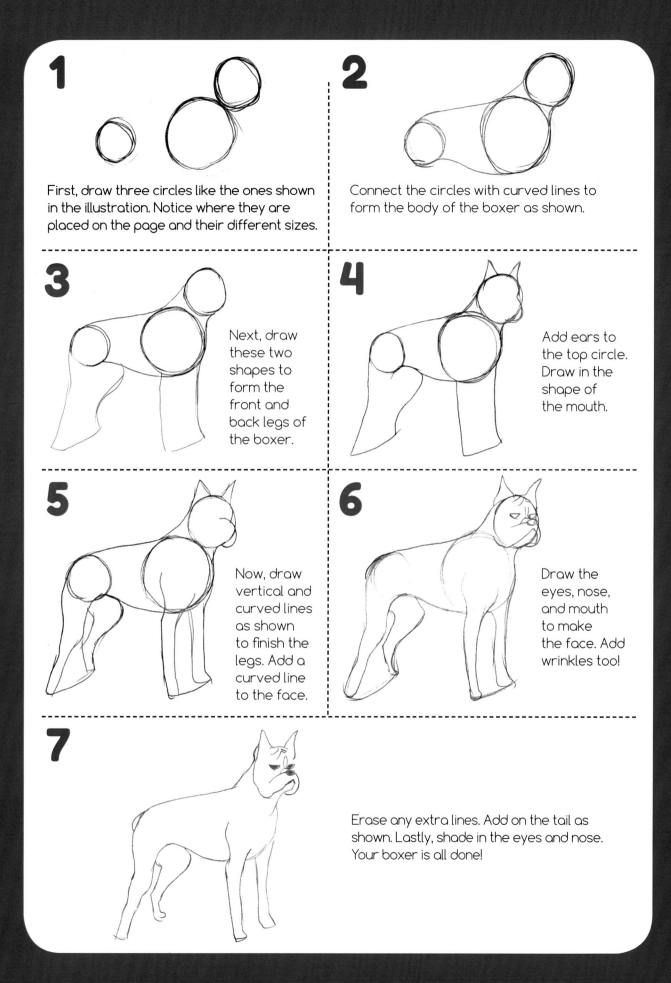

First, draw three circles like the ones shown in the illustration. Notice where they are placed on the page and their different sizes.

2

Connect the circles with curved lines to form the body of the boxer as shown.

3

Next, draw these two shapes to form the front and back legs of the boxer.

4

Add ears to the top circle. Draw in the shape of the mouth.

5

Now, draw vertical and curved lines as shown to finish the legs. Add a curved line to the face.

6

Draw the eyes, nose, and mouth to make the face. Add wrinkles too!

7

Erase any extra lines. Add on the tail as shown. Lastly, shade in the eyes and nose. Your boxer is all done!

GLOSSARY

ancestor: A relative who lived long ago.

breed: A group of animals that look alike and have the same kind of relatives.

conservation: Efforts to care for the natural world.

domesticated: Bred and raised for use by people.

ecosystem: All the living things in an area.

evolve: To develop and change over many years.

personality: How a person or animal acts in relation to others.

prey: An animal hunted by other animals for food.

technique: A particular skill or ability that someone uses to perform a job.

trait: A feature that makes an individual special.

yodel: To make a sound by changing from a natural voice to one much higher in pitch, and quickly back again.